PENGUIN MODERN POETS 5

The Penguin Modern Poets are succinct guides to the richness and diversity of contemporary poetry. Every volume brings together representative selections from the work of three poets now writing, allowing the curious reader and the seasoned lover of poetry to encounter the most exciting voices of our moment.

SAM RIVIERE was a recipient of a 2009 Eric Gregory Award, and his debut collection, *81 Austerities* (Faber & Faber, 2012), won the Forward Prize for Best First Collection. His second collection, *Kim Kardashian's Marriage*, followed from Faber in 2015. His standalone pamphlets include *Standard Twin Fantasy* (Egg Box Publishing, 2014) and *True Colours* (After Hours, 2016). *Safe Mode*, an ambient novel, is published by Test Centre (2017). He runs the limited edition poetry press If a Leaf Falls from Edinburgh, where he lives.

FREDERICK SEIDEL was born in St Louis and lives in New York City. His first book of poems, *Final Solutions*, initially won and then was denied the Young Men's and Young Women's Hebrew Association Poetry Prize amid controversy in 1962, before being published in New York the following year. The collections that followed are *Sunrise* (1980); *These Days* (1989); *My Tokyo* (1993); *Going Fast* (1998), a finalist for the Pulitzer Prize for Poetry; *The Cosmos Trilogy*, comprising *The Cosmos Poems* (2000), *Life on Earth* (2001) and *Area Code 212* (2002); *Ooga-Booga* (2006), which was a finalist for the National Book Critics Circle Award, was shortlisted for the International Griffin Poetry Prize, and won the *L. A. Times* Book Prize for Poetry; the limited edition chapbook *Evening Man* (2008); *Nice Weather* (2012); and *Widening Income Inequality* (2016). A *Selected Poems* was published by Faber & Faber in 2006. He received the PEN/Voelker Award for Poetry in 2002, and *The Paris Review*'s Hadada Award in 2014.

KATHRYN MARIS is originally from New York and has lived in London since 1999. Her poetry collections are *The Book of Jobs* (Four Way Books, 2006) and *God Loves You* (Seren, 2013). Her poetry has been published widely, including in *Granta, The Nation, The New Statesman, Poetry, The Best British Poetry 2015* (Salt) and *The Forward Book of Poetry 2017* (Faber & Faber). Her third collection, *The House with Only an Attic and a Basement*, will be published by Penguin in 2018.

MODERN POETS 5

Occasional Wild Parties

Sam Riviere

Frederick Seidel

Kathryn Maris

PENGUIN BOOKS

PENGUIN BOOKS

UK | USA | Canada | Ireland | Australia
India | New Zealand | South Africa

Penguin Books is part of the Penguin Random House group of companies
whose addresses can be found at global.penguinrandomhouse.com

This collection first published 2017
001

Set in Warnock Pro 9.65/12.75 pt
Typeset by Jouve (UK), Milton Keynes
Printed in Great Britain by Clays Ltd, St Ives plc

A CIP catalogue record for this book is available from the British Library

ISBN: 978–0–141–98707–1

www.greenpenguin.co.uk

MIX
Paper from
responsible sources
FSC® C018179

Penguin Random House is committed to a
sustainable future for our business, our readers
and our planet. This book is made from Forest
Stewardship Council® certified paper.

CONTENTS

Sam Riviere

from 81 Austerities

CRISIS POEM

In 3 years I have been awarded
£48,000 by various funding bodies
councils and publishing houses
for my contributions to the art
and I would like to acknowledge
the initiatives put in place
by the government and the rigorous
assessment criteria under which
my work has thrived since 2008
I have written 20 or 21 poems
developed a taste for sushi
decent wine bought my acquaintances
many beers many of whom have
never worked a day in their lives
how would you like to touch my palm
and divine how long my working
week has been mostly I watch films
and stare and try to decide what
to wear speaking as a poet I would
rather blow my brains out than run
out of credit as the biographer
of the famously unresolved
50s poet-suicide has commented
capital is the index of meaning
anything is better than stealing
from the Co-op with a clotted heart
without it you don't survive

THE SWEET NEW STYLE

she looks out of her
photo let's call her emma
with a mute appeal that might
mean something like 'whenever
you want just say I'm ready to be taken
away from all this' she is so shy
her eyes follow your eyes
over the girlish slopes and crests
hidden by her baggy cardigan jennifer
I mean emma let me assure you
your shyness has never been
so completely justified

DREAM POEM

I know what you're thinking
it's dull unless they're sex dreams
dreams about violent murders
mine are pretty banal
I dreamed I wrote a poem
beginning 'Hi!' and ending 'See You Later!'
the middle part was amazing
that's the part I don't remember
I was sitting on a platform high above the jungle
this all feels really familiar
probably from something I've seen on TV
I was dressed up as a witch doctor
and used this stick of judgement
taking back the names of creatures
restoring them to myth I was doing wisely with it
in my dream the poem didn't have
this assonance that's creeping in
after I'd taken back everything
I kept hold of my stick using it
to designate the categories that really matter
while adding bones and wings to my hat
sitting up here out of danger
I hate this / I like that

NO TOUCHING

I would like to ruin your life
let it not be said I lack the necessary
imagination to be jealous
I would ask you to tell no one about us
and if you tell no one about us
I'll fight hard to hide my disappointment
I would like you to renounce your past
as quite a big mistake
it will mean something although I
will never completely forgive you
I think you represent
the possibility in my life of renewal
I would like people to say
'she came back a different person'
we will appear at the weddings
of people we don't care about
our faces radiant from fucking

YEAR OF THE RABBIT

there is no purer form of advertising
than writing a poem
that's what the monk told me
if I were a conceptual artist
I would make high-budget trailers
of john updike novels but no actual movie
the scene where angstrom drives towards
the end of his life down a street in the suburbs
lined with a type of tree he's never bothered
to identify and laden with white blossoms
reflecting slickly in the windscreen
I would fade in the music
as the old song was fading out
keeping the backing vocals at the same distance
kind of balancing the silence
the word RABBIT appears in 10-foot trebuchet

THE COUNCIL OF GIRLS

Today I stand before you
uncertain of my guilt
of what I am accused
or should say sorry for
your eyes are screwed
like knots in wood
filled with the suggestive quiet
of trees gossiping telepathically
maybe it would help
if I recited in an Irish accent
or sang a little song
your faces grow more beautiful
as I am wired to the lie detector
crueller yet more pitying
I see there are hundreds of texts
to be read out and correlated
and I am happy to help as best I can
clear up this confusion
clarify and analyse the things I said
while drunk I speak to you
without the hope of mercy
you are everything to me
daughters
I kneel on the ground from which
you sprung
my jury of sunflowers

YOU THERE IN THE SHADOWS

come out where I can see you
through the dense mist of my cataracts
perhaps you bring me news of my daughter
who was married and shipped two moons ago
no perhaps then you have come bearing gifts a case
of the local grape of which in my later years I have become
inordinately fond no I can see from your expression I'm mistaken
ah you have brought the reply from the queen of Spain a resoun-
                                                          ding yes

PERSONAL STATEMENT

hi i should like to have the answers
to shall we say certain questions
and to wake up certain of directions
and a levelness of breathing and
of not being in a neo-noir movie
instead the mildness of the evening
and the possibility of ice-cream
waiting ahead in girlfriend heaven
when i return with gifts one chocolate
one strawberry i'll think of a question
any question the way you might prop
a stick below a window letting in
night air then pick that stick up from
its slant using it to gesture wisely
while elaborating on whatever
making all the time shall we say finer
distinctions splitting pairs of pairs
together like couples who both see
suddenly that this won't be for ever
it takes till now for the window to fall
and there can be no bitterness
or anger so what i'm saying is thank
you thank you and see you later

MY FACE SAW HER MAGAZINE

across the moonscapes of skateparks you are 13 yrs old
& no longer allowed to play with boys / on platform 6
wearing your amazing cape you are not in fact you
but someone else / while I'm a guy who mishears lyrics
resulting in a more beautiful but private understanding
with your dark fringe white shirt & straw hat you are
the palest goth at the picnic / resolutely uncharmed
by my very charming friend you are the poster of disinterest
in bed & matching underwear you are disguising the tunnel
we dug in the american prison / not answering my texts
what you are is the briefcase glowing with golden contents
I realise I can only look in one eye at a time / it is pure
propaganda the pupil a blot of blackest inkjet ink
in your luxury woollen garment you are an advertisement
for luxury woollen garments / & then & then you wink

from *Standard Twin Fantasy*

Sylvia taps a match on the rim of a big glass ashtray. Elizabeth
slides a finger down the inside cover of a magazine. Kimberly
weighs in her palm a marble egg. Weird harpsichord music plays.
Maude emerges from an oriental screen. Patricia flicks ash
into an oystershell. Bathsheba complicates the shadows
of a fern. Veronique angles the retro remote control
and leans against the massive fridge.

*

Standard twin fantasies are organized by the idea of duplication.
You meet A and E, gazing like a doubled void over their drinks.
Representatives of the same unknowable interior.
A has begun wearing a wristwatch on her left wrist.
You recognize E by the beauty mark she had removed,
and now replaces with a spot of black ink.

*

We go about our business like we're not being watched.
Such rooms do not exist: where shadows designate the villain,
curtains part to reveal a screen on which red curtains ripple.
And what should she be called, the woman framed always in the
window, in the television dust? Rooms that are the provinces of
ruined jokes. From which the afterlife appears as an ordinary
street. Where detectives go, for practice, between cases.

Best kiss (boys). Most cameod in garish dreams. Least drunk.
Last looked after after dark. Worst fake. First to get there late.
Last to stay. Most thought about in shortest thoughts.
The shortest shorts. Most surrounded by the kisses of jewellery
and loose change. Least fazed. Last to visit France. First to fire
a gun. The worst upstaged. The fewest words. Most often
caught. The favourite to escape. Most likely to think in flames.

*

That summer I trained myself to gaze upwards as I walked, into
the quiet gulf between the skyscrapers, letting my eyes adjust to
the sky's intensity. Its blue seemed to grow in strength and
simplicity the longer I looked, and I was able to wander for
hours with little awareness of the busy streets, my chin tilted up,
floating over the crossings in a kind of trance, my eyes filled with
clouds or the evening's grades. Crowds began to seem
comfortable, like surrounding trees, or a river's company. When
the sky lost definition, I'd drift into a restaurant, still carrying this
feeling of openness and freedom. I'd calmly eat, and wait for the
city to settle, restoring itself at new boundaries around me.

*

Amber Ashes. Plans to be much happier. Bridget Baleful.
Most overheard fake gasping. Cadence Circus. Remembered
haunting corridors. Deidre Debris. Will run a marathon
on love. Elsie Ectoplasm. Will stay up to watch the sunrise
once: a gradual brightening from black to grey. Faith
Phantasmagorical. Most likely to exit the waterslide unflowered.
Gina Gray. Most given flowers. I turned my back to talk.
Where I grew up, it took for ever. I'd spend my last dollar
on fireworks. How old am I, New York.

There was a time when headlights lit us up like guilt. What
the cameras asked, we answered. There was a time when
such heroines were punished. When we say we need
your help, we mean it's more than most men can afford. When
we offer you a peach, it is in black and white. When we say
our husband, we mean our dead husband. See the suburbs
in our sunglasses: in permanent night, in Italian night.

*

Standard twin fantasies are organized by the idea of repetition.
You meet A, and a week later mistake her for her twin, E.
It could be a relief, to live life as a plot device. As you leave
the room, she enters, swapping shoes, hairclips. Unlike a story,
this image has no ending. If you know me when I see you
you still haven't learnt to read.

*

Alice looks up, unsure how long you've been standing there.
There is a roughness in the atmosphere, like the friction when
a bet goes sour. You have just arrived, or are about to leave.
In this moment, she is less like a motive, more like a crime.
Less like a product, more like a sale. She is surrounded
by references that do not touch her. Like money.
She is about to smile or something.

from Kim Kardashian's Marriage

BEAUTIFUL POOL

The splendor of Florida's Gulf Coast
is rivalled by the elegant interior
of your luxurious two bedrooms.

Do you have a dream to build?
This image is minimalist.
Beautiful green grass scattered on the ground.

I really surprised myself
with several patios and intricate corridors,
antiques saved from around the world.

Like, I mean I knew I was that good.
I just didn't think I could do it
under that much pressure.

View images as 'a river of photos',
immaculate and perfect.

GRAVE SUNSETS

I said to her, now that is to my liking,
as clouds sail by golden-red,
aided by smoke from fuel-reduction burns
in the nearby forests.

From the first breath that you take
I'll be there for you.
We'll laugh until we have to cry.
I am familiar with the scenario,

the last home
of Hollywood icon Marilyn Monroe
and with their interpretation of the word.
Three days in the grave.

I don't wanna feel the emptiness.

THIRTY-THREE SINCERITY

Concerning the stupidity of evil,
commercial culture:
thirty-three poems.

Mary J. Blige:
twenty-two additional poems,
'the second of four children'.

A recapitulation of the formulation
of the aesthetic conflict:
fifty-two poems,

and a reformulation:
the fragrance's unprecedented success
broke sales records in hours.

At fifteen my heart was set on candour,
at thirty I stood learning
modern lyric poetry,

funeral prayer
firm hypocrisy.
At forty I had no opposite.

AMERICAN SINCERITY

Let us draw near to Russia.
Let us go right into the presence of film criticism.
Let us celebrate music since 2002.
Let us give out pies and eat corn dogs.

Jump to The Sound of Young America
with its undercurrents of guilty conscience.
We have been sprinkled with sauce by radio hosts,
not with the old blood,

nor with the speech espoused to make us clean,
not old D. H. Lawrence.
But even here we suspected as much.
It's now (a satire).

Therefore keep the network peace.
Therefore label the location,
with a heart in full idea,
with hearts fully defined in American English.

BEAUTIFUL SUNGLASSES

Since I am a model I have to think a lot

    inspiring picture

for my security and protection

    we heart it

I am keen in my profession so always
want to look best and presentable

    looking for cheap we supply cheap

Actress Nicollette Sheridan was enjoying
the beautiful beaches
of Saint Barts on Christmas Day wearing
the new Christian Dior
worn by Dimitra Spanou in 'Beautiful Greece'

    on background blue sky
    she looks like this and more

INFINITY BERRIES

Some years ago, it was.
I just ate some of those
things that make sour
sweet and my blood
powered a plain necklace.
I am trying to locate
variety and a feeling,
it is cushiony soft,
yet it's diamond
to the touch. Talk to me
bold in the morning.
You'll love the feather
tattooed on my flower.

BEAUTIFUL DUST

It's amazing what he could do,
Job is the one who said from dust
I came and the Lord taketh away.
Beautiful job!! Brings tears to my eyes.

A little sleepy, shy, neurotic guy,
this probably started with
wash me and those smiley faces,
a weakness for nebulae.

Yes, the Lord giveth but he
has come a long way since then.
Reserved, faithful, melancholy,
to dust I shall return. I have.

Which is not something you get
to say every day to those
that prefer to use their disguise.
Believer, enjoy this amazing dust.

INFINITY SINCERITY

For a guy who claims to hate cheesy stuff,
he proved true what he said before;
that for the girl he truly love,
he'll do anything possible to show.

All this while I've been loyal to LJ. Seriously.
LJ is very easy to manage. Just the html to edit,
hath thou forsaken me, that I am blind
and cannot see the simple truth

that dwells in me. They taught me how
to dodge and lie to hide my codes.
Cut and paste the here and there.
Forget what the intentions were . . .

Four brief years ago (it seems relevant)
I was a youth in college, but some of us
were looking at the Hummingbird Animal Totem.
I panicked and now I'm doing astrophysics.

GRAVE DUST

The night I got dust on my hands after dusting off my
  mother's grave.
I was lent a bass guitar for a while, and noodled in 7/8.
I heard the world's sounds whilst doing one of the early
  Alchemist's quests.
Your mother plays a significant role; that she is dead and gone
  has nothing to do with it.
So I jogged along to times and phrases gathered from
  mausoleums and sarcophagi.
I can concoct a thought to work in its usage. Didn't do
  anything with the results.
Too goddamn lazy to finish our page. I dislike the arts.

Preferences

People say olives are best served on ice, but I like them room temperature, in brine, unless it's warm enough to eat outside. I begin in the top left corner and proceed from left to right, pretty much in the way you'd imagine. I prefer watercolours of sportscars to an oil painting of dead people hunting. I include two luminous figures and a huge, black, church-like interior. I support the early work that supports an alternative reading. A figure of eight in the acres of parking. I'm not in favour of towns that bow down to their cemeteries. I sought my revenge in proxy realities. A nice panic attack in the midwinter market. My picture used to hang here, but I filled it in with block colour. This is the sixth reproduction. In practice it's costly, but it costs more than I spent. The moment I'm after is when one person in a crowd of thousands looks straight at the camera. Instead of a sentence you could just build a shelf. For the 40th time I died trying to break in to the collectors' convention. My city is custom, my language is custom, I built the maps from an ancient graveyard. I don't know my own number. I enjoy the music of ice cubes. When my prince came on a plane I heard his soft thunder. I searched for Los Angeles, and a few other places, but ended up here, in the one city they decided to raze. I relax by playing a stressful game. I want to see your side of the version. I praise the back of a painting. I see consciousness as a pond-shaped, deepening dip that I can feel myself occupy as I fall asleep. I had plans for words that never came to anything. I even had words for the storm's 'architecture'. I copied your notes. They just use rain to erase the tall buildings. We're not so different, the system and me. With all the huge ads and bouts of consumption I felt like I was in Britain or something. The boys stand without moving in tiny white cubicles, still believing they're being considered. The youth all have that Aryan look. If the talk is too boring I like to imagine Levin's pioneering use of the acronym. When cleaning a staircase I leave one step unswept, just to compare with. Everything I've ever loved fits in your silhouette. I get collector's envy. A glass breaks when I remember your name, but not because I remember your name. The shelves are all sanded, but it's a question in practice of deciding what not to put on them. Not this, it's too light. The sign says I'm out to meet an unplanned event. Please do not contact me with offers or services. For now my tribute remains this side of the virtual. I ran down the darkened passageway to receive my scar. I will never say this out loud.

Mindfulness

My friend had begun sending clips of blank walls overlaid
    with his maniacal laughter

Not quite summer

And crying in the Starbucks

You were recording the May riots

With dispiriting results

And there were hopes for a late

Light period

Even if most were already living like doomed celebrities

Holed up in discrete buildings

On the verge of perpetrating acts of artistic barbarism

I perceived a spoon as the title of a plate of food

Sweated the legacy of my centre parting

But we were all ailing

In the pallor of the decade

Some said that the abstract could save us

They called it new which was funny

And gathered in strong winds outside the hilltop residence
    of the famous DJ

While the sun went down

And harpies swooped off into the night . . .

You didn't want to be held

As the marathon diverged around us

Like everyone you were grappling with the now overwhelming
   realisation

That our session had expired

I chasmed

Between ordering

Those recycled seconds of empty hilarity

And the baristas chorusing our names together

Conscious Uncoupling

I wear the same clothes every day

Because every day I feel basically the same

Just some plain robes will be fine

And good luck trying to get a signal on Mount Sinai in this
weather

A friend registers an opportunity like a business

Offering limited access

But fuck that, I want the codes

The feeling of having a phone in each pocket

As I come down the hill with fresh updates

Sharing is totally passive aggressive

I really believe that

But I feel generous when smashing your fake tablets for the
bronze fragments

Even if the pictures depress me

I can profit

When a business leaves you

My iPhone is a poetic device

Severing contacts

And from the number its name

White Pizza

There comes a time when you stop even seeing McSweeney's
emails

In a landscape littered with large carapaces

Interns are wading through the slush sustained only by
bloody marys

Poetry doesn't make any sense

In a socialist utopia

But motherfucker this is Media City

And like a true bourgeois I love surveillance

In fact any aberrant behaviour consecrating the self

The least unique aspect of any person is their feelings

The interns agreed as I cancelled their contracts and bought
the quesadillas

This was the era before the end of analysis

And the theory of success as the deferral of pleasure

When I felt the schwing of fascism

Laying hungry and happy in a glade of wildflowers

Perfectly friendless

Still recovering from my twenty-five second obsession with
Teresa Oman

I experience an unexpected negation

Like a photographer at a permissible spectacle

When I find out she's Australian

True Colours

Straight white males only do disaffected don't they

I mean what else is there

Just so you know I'm sipping on an effervescent drink

A similar blue-yellow

To the eerie evening light that's currently

Planging off the suburbs

Where a day-moon waits to field it

Behind that line of bone-dry beach towels

Looking cheesier than ever

Just gusting on its anthem

And a breeze inflates my shorts

As too late I work out all my problems

Stem from dressing like I had black hair

Like I could somehow pull off green

Next time I look the moon has flaked or faded

The urge to take a picture departing long before it

And in agreement the pages of the hardback notebook

That I dare not write in riffle

Blueish

Nothing about them but their privilege

Christmas in Berlin

The woman in the advert has a look of knowingness that
    indicates an unspoken but completely real satisfaction

And I am certain that someone

Not her is getting away with something

A man was scorched to death in the shower

A dormant screen inspects the bed like a hypnotist

The Thai food almost left me angry enough to write a review

And I thought of my weirdo friend who collected figurines of
    Nazi skeletons with guns that stood on mounds of skulls

Though I never really worked out what he meant by them

The tennis I guess always makes me think of sex

Couldn't find the Palace of Tears again

And I felt far too nervous to ask

In case of more sad news

Please send nudes

In Praise of the Passivity of Paper

I felt suddenly convinced that I had feelings for the wallpaper.
I was especially captivated by its blonde hair and bad dreams.
I had the impression the wallpaper needed longer to properly respond.
By the time I left, my affections had produced this abrasion on my cheek.
People looked on the abrasion as unquestionable proof of my sincerity.
The abrasion was produced by rubbing my face on the paper's smooth surface.
It only occurred to me later that it may have found this sensation disagreeable.
But by then I had become known for my abrasion, and I seldom thought of,
discussed, or in any way depended upon the wallpaper for anything.
My affections, though, had produced upon the paper its own mark.
To my annoyance and eventual dismay, interest in the paper's abrasion
began to outweigh interest in my own; indeed, mine was starting to fade
while the mark upon the paper had deepened with the passing of time.
People liked to visit the paper in its room and probe their fingers
into the widening tear, by now a gruesome black-edged wound.
The silence of the paper during these incursions suggested to some
condemnation of their curiosity, but to others signalled its endorsement.
Some even speculated that the paper 'enjoyed' the infringement

of its surfaces, while most agreed it was a question of the paper enduring this indignity, having little or no opportunity to protest. Some visitors could not contain their enthusiasm, and over time other openings were fashioned in the paper without its consent. The earliest admirers of the paper's abrasion were heard lamenting the gulf between the paper's current state and its previous appearance. They opined that to experience the abrasion now was to encounter a kind of mockery of the gentle and informal gesture it had once been. Others contended that while the paper's condition was certainly different, it couldn't be in any way 'better' or 'worse' than it had been originally; on the contrary the paper, exhibiting as it did the marks of the affections spent upon it, was in every way a true record of the destruction this attention had wrought, and had become if anything a more moving testament, charting as it did the changing and accelerated passions of the times. In later phases of the paper's deterioration some expressed admiration for the stoical indifference with which the paper withstood its abusers and wondered if such an attitude might not improve the willing and reciprocal style with which they and their contemporaries were accustomed to giving and receiving each other's gazes and caresses. Against the odds, this view seemed timely and took root in the populace,

and to this day in all the estimations of historians and critics of culture
it is widely held accountable for the period of dormancy and inertia
among the youngest of our people, whose silence and repose
have replaced the humours and rages of those whose desires had flown
unchecked, who had coupled for so long with such energy and frequency.

You Must Leave All Your Belongings Behind

The airport where all movies end:
the scenery's mobile, the people too
(the people *want to be moved*),
and the rounded stairways join set pieces
like farewells in a series arc. I don't
understand how you write good scripts
without knowing there are gods. I've
learned the same things we've all learned:
when a man runs through my hotel suite
I can expect another half a second later.
Also, tell me why I keep two keys,
one of which unlocks something.
Also, I know, we know, that you (hell-*o*)
will have vanished before I finish saying this
and turn around. 'You'll do that,' I'll mention
to the night, and spin my swivel chair,
perusing the moment's sunkenness. Meanwhile
my antivirus angel is checking every file.
We both know there's a place you touch
when your plane lifts off (I won't say where),
a little bolt that takes the plot apart,
so closure is dismantled, because from here
you can admit that nothing's ever ended well.
You have queued to show your documents.
You have left behind your possessions
for the kind scientists. The stairs have spun
away and sunk, and in losing your itinerary
your position is confirmed. Like, the first time
a woman sees a diamond she just knows.

Solitaire

I think I always liked the game
because it sounded like my name
combined with the concept of alone.
(My name really does mean 'alone'
in Slovenian!) We don't actually care
if it's true, but we want to know
the person telling us is telling us
the truth. Say his name is 'Hank,'
as in, 'of hair.' (It's not.) My upbringing
was classically smooth/chaotic, apart
from traumatic events I've never detailed,
even to myself. Traumatic but methodical.
But why say what happened even.
In the tech block the blinds were down
and I cleared my way to the final marble
under the indistinct gaze of an indistinct
master. My success had allowed me
to become the bastard I always knew
I could be. What did it mean, to clean
the board like this, counting down to one?
By these gradual and orderly subtractions
my persona was configured. The goal
was to remain single. Sometimes telling you
the truth wouldn't be telling you anything
much. For a while I've felt torpid and detuned,
as if I want to share a view with you,
so we can both be absent in one place.
Look, the sky is beautiful and sour.
I'm not here, too. I'm staring out of this cloud
like an anagram whose solution
is probably itself. I am only the method
that this stupid game was invented to explain.

Frederick Seidel

Wanting to Live in Harlem

Pictures of violins in the Wurlitzer collection
Were my bedroom's one decoration,
Besides a blue horse and childish tan maiden by Gauguin –
Backs, bellies, and scrolls,
Stradivarius, Guarnerius, Amati,
Colored like a calabash-and-meerschaum pipe bowl's
Warmed, matured body –

The color of the young light-skinned colored girl we had then.
I used to dream about her often,
In sheets she'd have to change the day after.
I was thirteen, had just been bar mitzvah.
My hero, once I'd read about him,
Was the emperor Hadrian; my villain, Bar Kokhba,
The Jew Hadrian had crushed out at Jerusalem:

Both in the *Cambridge Ancient History*'s Hadrian chapter (1936
Edition), by some German. (The Olympics
Year of my birth and Jesse Owens's *putsch* it had appeared.)
Even then, in '49, my mother was dying.
Dressed in her fresh-air blue starched uniform,
The maid would come from Mother's room crying
With my mother's tears shining on her arm,

And run to grab her beads and crucifix and missal,
I to find my violin and tuning whistle
To practice my lessons. Mendelssohn. Or Bach,
Whose Lutheran fingering had helped pluck
The tonsured monks like toadstools from their lawns,
And now riddled the armor I would have to shuck:
His were life-sized hands behind his puppet Mendelssohn's.

One night, by the blue of her nitelite, I watched the maid
Weaving before her mirror in the dark, naked.
Her eyes rolled, whiskey-bright; the glass was black, dead.
'Will you come true? It's me, it's me,' she said.
Her hands and her hips clung to her rolling pelvis.
Her lips smacked and I saw her smile, pure lead
And silver, like a child, and shape a kiss.

All night I tossed. I saw the face,
The shoulders and the slight breasts – but a boy's face,
A soft thing tangled, singing, in his arms,
Singing and foaming, while his blinding pelvis,
Scooped out, streamed. His white eyes dreamed,
While the black face pounded with syncope and madness.
And then, in clear soprano, we both screamed.

What a world of mirrored darkness! Agonized, elated,
Again years later I would see it with my naked
Eye – see Harlem: doped up and heartless,
Loved up by heroin, running out of veins
And out of money and out of arms to hold it – where
I saw dead saplings wired to stakes in lanes
Of ice, like hair out cold in hair straightener.

And that wintry morning, trudging through Harlem
Looking for furnished rooms, I heard the solemn
Pedal-toned bowing of the Bach Chaconne.
I'd played it once! How many tears
Had shined on Mother's face since then?
Ten years! I had been trying to find a room ten years,
It seemed that day, and been turned down again and again.

No violin could thaw
The rickety and raw
Purple window I shivered below, stamping my shoes.
Two boys in galoshes came goose-stepping down
The sheer-ice long white center line of Lenox Avenue.
A blue-stormcoated Negro patrolman,
With a yellowing badge star, bawled at them. I left too.

I had given up violin and left St Louis,
I had given up being Jewish,
To be at Harvard just another
Greek nose in street clothes in Harvard Yard.
Mother went on half dying.
I wanted to live in Harlem. I was almost unarmored . . .
Almost alone – like Hadrian crying

As his death came on, 'Your Hadrianus
Misses you, Antinous,
Misses your ankles slender as your wrists,
Dear child. We want to be alone.
His back was the city gates of Rome.
And now Jerusalem is dust in the sun.
His skies are blue. He's coming, child, I come.'

Fucking

I wake because the phone is really ringing.
A singsong West Indian voice
In the dark, possibly a man's,
Blandly says, 'Good morning, Mr Seidel;
How are you feeling, God?'
And hangs up after my silence.

This is New York –
Some mornings five women call within a half hour.

In a restaurant, a woman I had just met, a Swede,
Three inches taller
Than I was among other things, and immensely
Impassive, cold,
Started to groan, very softly and husky voiced.
She said,
'You have utter control over me, and you know it.
I can't do anything about it.'
I had been asking her about her job.

One can spend a lifetime trying to believe
These things.

I think of A.,
Before she became Lady Q.,
Of her lovely voice, and her lovely name.
What an extraordinary new one she took
With her marriage vows,
Even as titles go, extra fictitious. And ah –

And years later, at her request, paying a call on the husband
To ask if I could take her out

Once more, once, m'lord, for auld lang syne. She still wanted
To run away;
And had,
Our snowed-in week in the Chelsea
Years before.
How had her plane managed to land?

How will my plane manage to land?

How wilt thy plane manage to land?

Our room went out sledding for hours
And only returned when we slept,
Finally, with it still snowing, near dawn.

I can remember her sex,
And how the clitoris was set.

Now on to London where the play resumes –
The scene when I call on the husband. But first,

In Francis Bacon's queer after-hours club,
Which one went to after
An Old Compton Street Wheeler's lunch,
A gentleman at the bar, while Francis was off pissing,
Looking straight at me, shouted
'Champagne for the Norm'!'
Meaning normal, heterosexual.

The place where I stayed,
The genteel crowded gloom of Jimmy's place,
Was England – coiled in the bars of an electric fire
In Edith Grove.

Piece by piece Jimmy sold off the Georgian silver.
Three pretty working girls were his lodgers.

Walking out in one direction, you were in
Brick and brown oppidan Fulham.
Walking a few steps the other way, you heard
Augustus John's many mistresses
Twittering in the local Finch's,
And a few steps further on, in the smart restaurants,
The young grandees who still said 'gels.'

There was a man named Pericles Belleville,
There is a man named Pericles Belleville,
Half American.

At a very formal dinner party,
At which I met the woman I have loved the most
In my life, Belleville
Pulled out a stirling silver-plated revolver
And waved it around, pointing it at people, who smiled.
One didn't know if the thing could be fired.

That is the poem.

Robert Kennedy

I turn from Yeats to sleep, and dream of Robert Kennedy,
Assassinated ten years ago tomorrow.
Ten years ago he was alive –
Asleep and dreaming at this hour, dreaming
His wish-fulfilling dreams.
He reaches from the grave.

Shirtsleeves rolled up, a boy's brown hair, ice eyes
Softened by the suffering of others, and doomed;
Younger brother of a murdered president,
Senator and candidate for president;
Shy, compassionate and fierce
Like a figure out of Yeats;
The only politician I have loved says *You're dreaming* and says
The gun is mightier than the word.

The Blue-Eyed Doe

I look at Broadway in the bitter cold,
The center strip benches empty like today,
And see St Louis. I am often old
Enough to leave my childhood, but I stay.

A winter sky as total as repression
Above a street the color of the sky;
A sky the same grey as a deep depression;
A boulevard the color of a sigh:

Where Waterman and Union met was the
Apartment building I'm regressing to.
My key is in the door; I am the key;
I'm opening the door. I think it's true

Childhood is your mother even if
Your mother is in hospitals for years
And then lobotomized, like mine. A whiff
Of her perfume; behind her veil, her tears.

She wasn't crying anymore. Oh try.
No afterward she wasn't anymore.
But yes she will, she is. Oh try to cry.
I'm here – right now I'm walking through the door.

The pond was quite wide, but the happy dog
Swam back and forth called by the boy, then by
His sister on the other side, a log
Of love put-putting back and forth from fry

To freeze, from freeze to fry, a normal pair
Of the extremes of normal, on and on.
The dog was getting tired; the children stare –
Their childhood's over. Everything is gone,

Forest Park's deserted; still they call.
It's very cold. Soprano puffs of breath,
Small voices calling in the dusk is all
We ever are, pale speech balloons. One death,

Two ghosts . . . white children playing in a park
At dusk forever – but we must get home.
The mica sidewalk sparkles in the dark
And starts to freeze – or fry – and turns to foam.

At once the streetlights in the park go on.
Gas hisses from the trees – but it's the wind.
The real world vanishes behind the fawn
That leaps to safety while the doe is skinned.

The statue of Saint Louis on Art Hill,
In front of the museum, turns into
A blue-eyed doe. Next it will breathe. Soon will
Be sighing, dripping tears as thick as glue.

Stags do that when the hunt has cornered them.
The horn is blown. Bah-ooo. Her mind a doe
Which will be crying soon at bay. The stem
Between the autumn leaf and branch lets go.

My mother suddenly began to sob.
If only she could do that now. Oh try.
I feel the lock unlock. Now try the knob.
Sobbed uncontrollably. Oh try to cry.

How easily I can erase an error,
The typos my recalling this will cause,
But no correcting key erases terror.
One ambulance attendant flashed his claws,

The other plunged the needle in. They squeeze
The plunger down, the brainwash out. Bah-ooo.
Calm deepened in her slowly. There, they ease
Her to her feet. White Goddess, blond, eyes blue –

Even from two rooms away I see
The blue, if that is possible! Bright white
Of the attendants; and the mystery
And calm of the madonna; and my fright.

I flee, but to a mirror. In it, they
Are rooms behind me in our entrance hall
About to leave – the image that will stay
With me. My future was behind me. All

The future is a mirror in which they
Are still behind me in the entrance hall,
About to leave – and if I look away
She'll vanish. Once upon a time, a fall

So long ago that they were burning leaves,
Which wasn't yet against the law, I looked
Away. I watched the slowly flowing sleeves
Of smoke, the blood-raw leaf piles being cooked,

Sweet-smelling scenes of mellow preparation
Around a bloodstained altar, but instead
Of human sacrifice, a separation.
My blue-eyed doe! The severed blue-eyed head!

The windows were wide-open through which I
Could flee to nowhere – nowhere meaning how
The past is portable, and therefore why
The future of the past was always now

A treeless Art Hill gleaming in the snow,
The statue of Saint Louis at the top
On horseback, blessing everything below,
Tobogganing the bald pate into slop.

Warm sun, blue sky; blond hair, blue eyes; of course
They'll shave her head for the lobotomy,
They'll cut her brain, they'll kill her at the source.
When she's wheeled out, blue eyes are all I see.

The bandages – down to her eyes – give her
A turbaned Twenties look, but I'm confused.
There were no bandages. I saw a blur.
They didn't touch a hair – but I'm confused.

I breathe mist on the mirror . . . I am here –
Blond hair I pray will darken till it does,
Blue eyes that will need glasses in a year –
I'm here and disappear, the boy I was . . .

The son who lifts his sword above Art Hill;
Who holds it almost like a dagger but
In blessing, handle up, and not to kill;
Who holds it by the blade that cannot cut.

Vermont

The attitude of green to blue is love.
And so the day just floats itself away.
The stench of green, the drench of green, above
The ripples of sweet swimming in a bay
Of just-mowed green, intoxicates the house.
The meadow goddess squeaking like a mouse
Is stoned, inhales the grass, adores the sky.
The nostrils feed the gods until the eye
Can almost see the perfume pour the blue.
A Botticelli ladled from a well,
Your life is anything you want it to –
And loves you more than it can show or tell.

Racine

When civilization was European,
I knew every beautiful woman
In the Grand Hôtel et de Milan,
Which the Milanese called 'The Millin',
Where Verdi died, two blocks from La Scala,
And lived in every one of them
Twenty-some years ago while a motorcycle was being made
For me by the MV Agusta
Racing Department in Cascina Costa,
The best mechanics in the world
Moonlighting for me after racing hours.
One of the 'Millin' women raced cars, a raving beauty.
She owned two Morandis, had met Montale.
She recited verses from the Koran
Over champagne in the salon and was only eighteen
And was too good to be true.
She smilingly recited Leopardi in Hebrew.
The most elegant thing in life is an Italian Jew.
The most astonishing thing in life to be is an Italian Jew.
It helps if you can be from Milan, too.
She knew every *tirade* in Racine
And was only eighteen.
They thought she was making a scene
When she started declaiming Racine.
Thunderbolts in the bar.
With the burning smell of Auschwitz in my ear.
With the gas hissing from the ceiling.
Racine raved on racing tires at the limit of adhesion.
With the gas hissing from the showers.
I remember the glamorous etching on the postcard
The hotel continued to reprint from the original 1942 plate.
The fantasy hotel and street

Had the haughty perfect ease of haute couture,
Chanel in stone. A tiny tailored doorman
Stood as in an architectural drawing in front of the façade and
    streamlined
Cars passed by.
The cars looked as if they had their headlights on in the rain,
In the suave, grave
Milanese sunshine.

Kill Poem

Huntsman indeed is gone from Savile Row,
And Mr Hall, the head cutter.
The red hunt coat Hall cut for me was utter
Red melton cloth thick as a carpet, cut just so.
One time I wore it riding my red Ducati racer – what a show! –
Matched exotics like a pair of lovely red egrets.
London once seemed the epitome of no regrets
And the old excellence one used to know
Of the chased-down fox bleeding its stink across the snow.

We follow blindly, clad in coats of pink,
A beast whose nature is to run and stink.
I am civilized in my pink but
Civilized is about having stuff.
The red coats are called 'pinks'. Too much is almost enough.
No one knows why they are. I parade in the air
With my stuff and watch the disappearing scut
Of a deer. I am civilized but
Civilized life is actually about too much.

I parade in the air
And wait for the New Year
That then will, then will disappear.
I am trying not to care.
I am not able not to.
A short erect tail
Winks across the winter field.
All will be revealed.
I am in a winter field.

They really are everywhere.
They crawl around in one's intimate hair.

They spread disease and despair.
They rape and pillage
In the middle of Sag Harbor Village.
They ferry Lyme disease.
The hunters' guns bring them to their knees.
In Paris I used to call the Sri Lankan servants 'Shrees.'
I am not able not to.

Winter, spring, Baghdad, fall,
Venery is written all
Over me like a rash,
Hair and the gash,
But also the Lehrer *NewsHour* and a wood fire and Bach.
A short erect tail
Winks across the killing field.
All will be revealed.
I am in a killing field.

I remember the *chasse à courre* in the forest in the Cher.
I remember the English thoroughbreds ridden by the frogs.
I remember the weeping stag cornered by the dogs.
The stag at bay in the pond literally shed a tear.
A hunt servant in a tricorn hat waded out to cut its throat.
Nelson Aldrich on his horse vomited watching this.
The huntsman's heraldic horn sounded the *hallali*.
The tune that cuts off the head. *L'hallali!*
Back to the château to drink the blood. *L'hallali!*

I am in Paris being introduced at Billy's,
1960, avenue Paul-Valéry.
One of her beautiful imported English Lillys or Millys
Is walking around on her knees.
It is rather like that line of Paul Valéry's.
Now get down on all fours, please.

We are ministers of state and then there is me chez Billy.
Deer garter-belt across our field of vision
And stand there waiting for our decision.

Our only decision was how to cook the venison.
I am civilized but
I see the silence
And write the words for the thought balloon.
When the woods are the color of a macaroon,
Deer, death is near.
I write about its looks in my books.
I write disappearing scut.
I write rut.

The title is *Kill Poetry*,
And in the book poetry kills.
In the poem the stag at bay weeps, literally.
Kill poetry is the *hallali* on avenue Paul-Valéry.
Get rid of poetry. Kill poetry.
Label on a vial of pills. Warning: Kill kill kill kills.
Its title is *Kill Poem*,
From the *Book of Kills*.
The antlered heads are mounted weeping all around the walls.

John F. Kennedy is mounted weeping on the wall.
His weeping brother Robert weeps nearby.
Martin Luther King, at bay in Memphis, exhausted, starts to cry.
His antlered head is mounted weeping on the wall.
Too much is almost enough, for crying out loud!
Bobby Kennedy announces to the nighttime crowd
That King has died, and then quotes Aeschylus, and then is killed.
Kill kill kill kills, appalls,
The American trophies covered in tears that deck the
    American halls.

Poem Does

The god in the nitroglycerin
Is speedily absorbed under the tongue
Till it turns a green man red,
Which is what a poem does.
It explosively reanimates
By oxygenating the tribe.

No civilized state will execute
Someone who is ill
Till it makes the someone well
Enough to kill
In a civilized state,
As a poem does.

I run-and-bump the tiny
Honda 125cc Grand Prix racer. Only
Two steps and it screams. I
Slip the clutch to get the revs up, blipping and getting
Ready not to get deady,
Which also is what a poem does.

They dress them up in the retirement centers.
They dress them up in racing leathers.
They dress them up in war paint and feathers.
The autumn trees are in their gory glory.
The logs in the roaring fire keep passing
The peace pipe in pain, just what a poem does.

Stanza no. 5. We want to be alive.
Line 26. We pray for peace.
Line 27. The warrior and peacemaker Rabin is in heaven.
28. We don't accept his fate.
But we do. Life is going ahead as fast as it can,
Which is what a poem does.

Barbados

Literally the most expensive hotel in the world
Is the smell of rain about to fall.
It does the opposite, a grove of lemon trees.
I isn't anything.
It is the hooks of rain
Hovering with their sweets inches above the ground.
I is the spiders marching through the air.
The lines dangle the bait
The ground will bite.
Your wife is as white as vinegar, pure aristo privilege.
The excellent smell of rain before it falls overpowers
The last aristocrats on earth before the asteroid.
I sense your disdain, darling.
I share it.

The most expensive hotel in the world
Is the African slave ship unloading Africans on the moon.
They wear the opposite of space suits floating off the dock
To a sugar mill on a hilltop.
They float into the machinery.
The machine inside the windmill isn't vegetarian.
A 'lopper' lops off a limb caught
In the rollers and the machine never has to stop.
A black arm turns into brown sugar,
And the screaming rest of the slave keeps the other.
His African screams can't be heard above the roar.
A spaceship near the end of a voyage was becalmed.
Two astronauts floated weightlessly off the deck
Overboard into the equator in their chains and *splash* and
    drowned.

A cane toad came up to them.
They'd never seen anything so remarkable.
Now they could see the field was full of them.
Suddenly the field is filled with ancestors.
The hippopotamuses became friendly with the villagers.
Along came white hunters who shot the friendly hippos dead.
If they had known that friendship would end like that,
They would never have entered into it.
Suddenly the field is filled with souls.
The field of sugarcane is filled with hippopotamus cane toads.
They always complained
Our xylophones were too loud.
The Crocodile King is dead.
The world has no end.

The crocodile explodes out of the water and screams at the crowd
That one of them has stolen his mobile phone.
On the banks of the muddy Waddo, *ooga-booga!*
What about a Christmas tree in a steamy lobby on the Gulf of
    Guinea!
Because in Africa there are Africans
And they are Africans and are in charge.
Even obstipation
Can't stop a mighty nation.
The tragic magic makes lightning.
Some of the young captives are unspeakable
In their beauty, and their urine makes lightning, black and gold.
The heat is so hot
It will boil you in a pot.
Diarrhea in a condom is the outcome.

The former president completely loses it and screams from
    the stage
That someone fucking stole his fucking phone.
The audience of party faithful is terrified and giggles.
This was their man who brought the crime rate down
By executing everyone.
The crocodile staged a coup
And ended up in prison himself
And then became the president.
He stood for quality of life and clitorectomy.
But in his second term, in order to secure those international
    loans,
The crocodile changed his spots to free speech.
Lightning sentences them at birth to life without parole
With no time off for good behavior.
At that point in the voyage the ocean turns deeper.

People actually suffered severe optical damage from the
    blinding effects
Of the white roads in full sunlight.
It is the island roads so white you can't see,
Made of crushed limestone snow.
It is the tropical rain the color of a grapefruit
Hovering in the figure of the goddess Niscah
Above the tile roof of the plantation house.
She dangles her baited lines.
It is the black of the orchids in a vase.
The goddess overpowers the uprising
And *I* is the first one hacked to pieces.
The asteroid is coming to the local cinema.
It is a moonlit night with the smell of rain in the air.
Thump thump, speed bump.

The most expensive hotel in the world ignites
As many orgasms as there are virgins in paradise.
These epileptic foaming fits dehydrate one,
But justify the cost of a honeymoon.
The Caribbean is room temperature,
Rippling over sand as rich as cream.
The beach chair has the thighs of a convertible with the top
    down.
You wave a paddle and the boy
Runs to take your order.
Many things are still done barefoot.
Others have the breakout colors of a parrot.
In paradise it never rains, but smells as if it could.
Two who could catapulted themselves overboard into the
    equator.
I die of thirst and drown in chains, in love.

Into the coconut grove they go. *Into the coconut grove they go.*
The car in the parking lot is theirs. *The car in the parking lot
    is theirs.*
The groves of lemon trees give light. *Ooga-booga!*
The hotel sheds light. *Ooga-booga!*
The long pink-shell sky of meaning wanted it to be, but really,
The precious thing is that they voted. *Ooga-booga!* And there
    we were,
The cane toads and the smell of rain about to fall.
The crocodiles and spiders are
The hippos and their friends who shot them dead.
The xylophone is playing too loud
Under the coconut palms, which go to the end of the world.
The slave is screaming too loud and we
Can't help hearing
Our tribal chant and getting up to dance under the
    mushroom cloud.

Climbing Everest

The young keep getting younger, but the old keep
    getting younger.
But this young woman is young. We kiss.
It's almost incest when it gets to this.
This is the consensual, national, metrosexual
    hunger-for-younger.

I'm getting young.
I'm totally into strapping on the belt of dynamite
Which will turn me into light.
God is great! I suck Her tongue.

I mean – my sunbursts, and there are cloudbursts.
My dynamite penis
Is totally into Venus.
My penis in Venus hungers and thirsts,

It burns and drowns.
My dynamite penis
Is into Venus.
The Atlantic off Sagaponack is freezing black today and frowns.

I enter the jellyfish folds
Of floating fire.
The mania in her labia can inspire
Extraordinary phenomena and really does cure colds.

It holds the Tower of Pisa above the freezing black waves.
The mania is why
I mention I am easily old enough to die,
And actually it's the mania that saves

The Tower from falling over.
Climbing Everest is a miracle – which leaves the descent
And reporting to the world from an oxygen tent
In a soft pasture of cows and clover.

Happening girls parade around my hospice bed.
The tented canopy means I am in the rue de Seine in Paris.
It will embarrass
Me in Paris to be dead.

It's Polonius embarrassed behind the arras,
And the arras turning red.
Hamlet has outed Polonius and Sir Edmund Hillary will wed
Ophelia in Paris.

Give me Everest or give me death.
Give me an altitude with an attitude.
But I am naked and nude.
I am constantly out of breath.

A naked woman my age is just a total nightmare,
But right now one is coming through the door
With a mop, to mop up the cow flops on the floor.
She kisses the train wreck in the tent and combs his white hair.

Broadway Melody

A naked woman my age is a total nightmare.
A woman my age naked is a nightmare.
It doesn't matter. One doesn't care.
One doesn't say it out loud because it's rare
For anyone to be willing to say it,
Because it's the equivalent of buying billboard space to display it,

Display how horrible life after death is,
How horrible to draw your last breath is,
When you go on living.
I hate the old couples on their walkers giving
Off odors of love, and in City Diner eating a ray
Of hope, and then paying and trembling back out on Broadway,

Drumming and dancing, chanting something nearly unbearable,
Spreading their wings in order to be more beautiful and more
    terrible.

Arnaut Daniel

'fictio rethorica musicaque poita'
— *Dante*, De vulgari eloquentia

A shiver of lightning buckles the sidewalk.
Love cracks my sternum open
In order to operate,
Lays bare the heart, pours in sugar and chalk.
I open my mouth unable to talk.
I am someone having a bleed or a stroke.

I never stop talking,
Never lose consciousness,
Dying to be charming.
I stand there at liftoff
Burning lightning,
Basically blasting from the launch pad to kingdom come.

I am running in place on fire on a high wire,
Running into you in the shop,
And then outside
Can't stop. You have just come from a spin class—
O lovely smile miles away, that doesn't stop not
Coming closer.

Age is a factor.
A Caucasian male nine hundred years old
Is singing to an unattainable lady, fair beyond compare,
Far above his pay grade, in front of Barzini's on Broadway,
In Provençal, or it's called Occitan, pronounced *oksitan*,
    or it's that
I am someone else, whoever else I am.

Ezra Pound channeling the great troubadour poet Arnaut Daniel
In St Elizabeths Hospital for the criminally insane
In Washington, D.C.,
Thanksgiving weekend, 1953,
I remember sounded like he
Was warbling words of birdsong.

One Last Kick for Dick

In memory of Richard Poirier (1925–2009)

Old age is not for sissies but death is just disgusting.
It's a dog covering a bitch, looking so serious, looking
   ridiculous, thrusting.
The EMS team forces a tube down your airway where blood is
   crusting.
Imagine internal organs full of gravel oozing and rusting.
An ancient vase crossing the street on a walker, trudgingly
   trusting
The red light won't turn green, falls right at the cut in the
   curb, bursting, busting.
The windshield wipers can't keep up. The wind is gusting.
A massive hemmorrhagic bleed in the brain stem is Emerson
   readjusting.

Why did the fucker keep falling?
I'm calling you. Why don't you hear me calling?
Why did his faculties keep failing?
I'm doing my usual schtick with him and ranting and railing.
You finally knocked yourself unconscious and into the next
   world
Where Ralph Waldo Emerson, in the ballroom of the mind,
   whirled and twirled.
Fifty-three years ago, at the Ritz in Boston, we tried one
   tutorial session in the bar.
You got so angry you kicked me under the table. Our martinis
   turned black as tar.
And all because your tutee told you Shakespeare was
   overrated. I went too far.

The Death of the Shah

Here I am, not a practical man,
But clear-eyed in my contact lenses,
Following no doubt a slightly different line than the others,
Seeking sexual pleasure above all else,
Despairing of art and of life,
Seeking protection from death by seeking it
On a racebike, finding release and belief on two wheels,
Having read a book or two,
Having eaten well,
Having traveled not everywhere in sixty-seven years but far,
Up the Eiffel Tower and the Leaning Tower of Pisa
And the World Trade Center Twin Towers
Before they fell,
Mexico City, Kuala Lumpur, Accra,
Tokyo, Berlin, Teheran under the Shah,
Cairo, Bombay, L.A., London,
Into the jungles and the deserts and the cities on the rivers
Scouting locations for the movie,
A blue-eyed white man with brown hair,
Here I am, a worldly man,
Looking around the room.

Any foal in the kingdom
The Shah of Iran wanted
He had brought to him in a military helicopter
To the palace.
This one was the daughter of one of his ministers, all legs,
    a goddess.
She waited in a room.
It was in the afternoon.

I remember mounds of caviar before dinner
In a magnificent torchlit tent,
An old woman's beautiful house, a princess,
Three footmen for every guest,
And a man who pretended to get falling-down drunk
And began denouncing the Shah,
And everyone knew was a spy for the Shah.

A team of New York doctors (mine among them)
Was flown to Mexico City to consult.
They were not allowed to examine the Shah.
They could ask him how he felt.

The future of psychoanalysis
Is a psychology of surface.
Stay on the outside side.
My poor analyst
Suffered a stroke and became a needy child.
As to the inner life: let the maid.

How pathetic is a king who died of cancer
Rushing back after all these years to consult more doctors.
Escaped from the urn of his ashes in his pajamas.
Except in Islam you are buried in your body.
The Shah mounts the foal.
It is an honor.
He is in and out in a minute.
She later became my friend
And married a Texan.

I hurry to the gallery on the last day of the show
To a line stretching around the block in the rain –
For the Shah of sculptors, sculpture's virile king,
And his cold-rolled steel heartless tons.

The blunt magnificence stuns.
Cruelty has a huge following.
The cold-rolled steel mounts the foal.

The future of psychoanalysis is it has none.
I carry a swagger stick.
I eat a chocolate.
I eat brown blood.

When we drove with our driver on the highways of Ghana
To see for ourselves what the slave trade was,
Elmina was Auschwitz.
The slaves from the bush were marched to the coast
And warehoused in dungeons under St George's Castle,
Then FedExed to their new jobs far away.

One hotel kept a racehorse as a pet.
The owner allowed it the run of the property.
Very shy, it walked standoffishly
Among the hotel guests on the walkways and under the palms.
The Shah had returned as a racehorse dropping mounds
    of caviar
Between a coconut grove and the Gulf of Guinea.

An English royal is taught to strut
With his hands clasped behind his back.
A racehorse in West Africa kept as a pet
Struts the same way the useless royals do,
Nodding occasionally to indicate he is listening.
His coat has been curried until he is glistening.

Would you rather be a horse without a halter
Than one winning races being whipped?
The finish line is at the starting gate, at St George's Castle.

The starting gate is at the finish line for the eternal life.
God rears and whinnies and gives a little wave.
He would rather be an owner than a slave.

Someone fancy says
How marvelous money is.
Here I am, an admirer of Mahatma Gandhi,
Ready to praise making pots of money
And own a slave.
I am looking in the mirror as I shave the slave.
I shave the Shah.
I walk into the evening and start being charming.

A counterfeiter prints me.
(The counterfeiter *is* me.)
He prints Mohammad Reza Shah Pahlavi.

I call him Nancy.
He is so fancy.
It is alarming
He is so charming.
It is the thing he does and knows.
It is the fragrance of a rose.
It is the nostrils of his nose.

It is the poetry and prose.
It is the poetry.
It is a horse cab ride through Central Park when it snows.
It is Jackie Kennedy's hairpiece that came loose,
That a large Secret Service agent helped reattach.

I remember the Duck and Duckess of Windsor.
You could entertain them in your house.

Here I am, looking around the room
At everyone getting old except the young,
Discovering that I am lacking in vanity,
Not that I care, being debonair,
Delighted by an impairment of feeling
That keeps everything away,
People standing around in a display case
Even when they are in bed with you,
And laser-guided bombs destroy the buildings
Inside the TV, not that I care,
Not that I do not like it at all,
Not that I am short or tall,
Not that I do not like to be alive,
And I appeal to you for pity,
Having in mind that you will read this
Under circumstances I cannot imagine
A thousand years from now.

Have pity on a girl, perdurable, playful,
And delicate as a foal, dutiful, available,
Who is waiting on a bed in a room in the afternoon for God.
His Majesty is on his way, who long ago has died.
She is a victim in the kingdom, and is proud.
Have pity on me a thousand years from now when we meet.
Open the mummy case of this text respectfully.
You find no one inside.

City

Right now, a dog tied up in the street is barking
With the grief of being left,
A dog bereft.
Right now, a car is parking.

The dog emits
Petals of a barking flower and barking flakes of snow
That float upward from the street below
To where another victim sits:

Who listens to the whole city
And the dog honking like a fire alarm,
And doesn't mean the dog any harm,
And doesn't feel any pity.

Sunset at Swan Lake

> 'My little girl is singing: Ah! Ah! Ah! Ah! I do not under-
> stand the meaning of this, but I feel its meaning. She wants
> to say that everything Ah! Ah! is not horror but joy.'
>   – *Nijinsky's* Diary

Nijinsky wants to be Nijinsky's body double. Nijinsky wants to
    splash in puddles.
He wants to rip the roof off and let the rain in and Ukraine in
    and be sane in.
Diaghilev and the rest of our kindergarten class will get soaked.
Windows and windshields – do you understand it's raining!
Headlights on in the daytime in the May warm rain
And lights on sweetly in the darkened living room
Feels like what it feels like staying home,
The music turned down low and cars hissing through the pain.
God asks the mirror: 'I don't have the emotional depth other
    people do, do you?'
He never wanted to, though he wanted to.
God stares into the full-length mirror in the foyer –
The border guard at the checkpoint stares back.
The guard won't let him enter the mirror.
'I only have one feeling and you've hurt my feeling!'

France Now

I slide my swastika into your lubricious Place Clichy.
I like my women horizontal and when they stand up vicious
    and Vichy.
I want to jackboot rhythmically down your Champs-Élysées
With my behind behind me taking selfies of the Grand Palais.
Look at my arm raised in the razor salute of greeting.
I greet you like a Caesar, *Heil!* for our big meeting.
My open-topped Mercedes creeps through the charming,
    cheering crowd.
I greet you, lovely body of Paris, you who are so proud,
And surtout you French artists and French movie stars who
Are eager to collaborate and would never hide a Jew.

My oh my. How times have changed.
But the fanatics have gotten even more deranged.
Seventy-five years after Hitler toured charming, cheering
    Paris, Parisians say
They won't give in to terrorist tyranny, and yesterday
Two million people marched arm in arm, hand in hand,
After the latest murderous horror, to take a stand
Against the latest fascist Nazi Islamist jihadi blasphemous
    horror and murder.
Absurd is getting absurder.
It's absurd in France to be a Jew
Because someone will want to murder you –

Someone who spreads infidel blood all over the walls and
    floor like jam –
Someone who, like you, doesn't eat ham.
He/she activates his/her suicide vest.
Children just out of the nest
Wearing a suicide vest

Are the best.

It's alarming

And queer to read Osama bin Laden writing an essay about
global warming.

So he was also human, like the ISIS fighters writing

Poems in the manner of the great pre-Islamic odes in the
midst of the fighting.

We are the Marseillaise. We are la civilisation française. Make
no mistake,

Civilization is at stake.

We are a paper frigate sailing on a burning lake –

Many decks and sails, and white and fancy as a wedding cake.

Listen. The Mu'allaqa of Imru' al-Qays, the *Iliad* of the Arabs,
keeps singing

In the desert, 'Come, let us weep,' while the bells of Notre-
Dame keep ringing

With alarm. In one of the Hadith,

Muhammad crowns me with a wreath

But damns me for eternity, Imru' al-Qays, and Labīd as well,

But me especially as the most poetic of poets and their leader
into hell.

Me

The fellow talking to himself is me,
Though I don't know it. That's to say, I see
Him every morning shave and comb his hair
And then lose track of him until he starts to care,
Inflating sex dolls out of thin air
In front of his computer, in a battered leather chair
That needs to be thrown out . . . then I lose track
Until he strides along the sidewalk on the attack
With racist, sexist outbursts. What a treat
This guy is, glaring at strangers in the street!
Completely crazy but not at all insane.
He's hot but there's frostbite in his brain.
He's hot but freezing cold, and oh so cool.
He's been called a marvelously elegant ghoul.

But with a torn rotator cuff, even an elegant fawn
Has to go through shoulder seizures to get his jacket on.
He manages spastically. His left shoulder's gone.
It means, in pain, he's drastically awake at dawn.
A friend of his with pancreatic cancer, who will die,
Is not in pain so far, and she will try
To palliate her death, is what her life is now.
The fellow's thinking to himself, Yes but how?
Riding a motorcycle very fast is one way to.
The moon and stars rapidly enter you
While you excrete the sun. You ride across the earth
Looking for a place to lay the eggs of your rebirth.
The eggs crack open and out comes everyone.
The chicks chirp, and it's begun, and it's fun.

You keep on writing till you write yourself away,
And even after – when you're nothing – you still stay.

The eggs crack open and out comes everyone.
The chicks chirp, the poems speak – and it's again begun!
Speaking of someone else for a change, not me,
There was that time in Stockholm when, so strangely,
Outside a restaurant, in blinding daylight, a tiny bird
Circled forever around us and then without a word
Lightly, lightly landed on my head and settled there
And you burst into tears. I was unaware
That ten years before the same thing had happened just
After your young daughter died and now it must
Have been Maria come back from the dead a second time
  to speak
And receive the recognition we all seek.

Miss Charlotte

Bring back the all-girls boarding schools for pedigreed girls
Where, morning and night, girls dressed and undressed.
Luxurious lawns and trees rode to hounds.
Horses the girls owned waited in padded stalls.

Think of the cold showers these aristocrats took.
Think of the dorm-room mirrors which sometimes saw
A cold girl lying on top of a warm girl
While a pretty girl with a pimply face on her bed on her back
    watched.

Have two rules, Miss Charlotte said:
Hard, good work and much fun.
She was addressing two favorites, Grits and little Bun-Bun.
There was gymkhana and dressage and raising the flag
    and French.

Keep up with the times, Miss Charlotte said. *Don't be narrow.*
Pick up on traditions and remember,
With God all things are possible.
On, on, with Foxcroft. Dare not let her die.

These ballgowns were tomboys who curtsy and bow.
These tigers were geldings life milks like a cow.
In life's cotillion, girls had to learn how
To be kapos at Dachau.

Kapos at Dachau, kapos at Dachau,
And pigeon-shooting on horseback at their plantations.
Once upon a time, du Pont, Mellon, Frick, Whitney, Astor . . .
Astor was a disaster.

What got into Bun-Bun Astor
To make Miss Charlotte, who loved her, walk right past her?
Each child learned how to be her horse's master
And complete the dressage routine a little faster.

Night softly turns into light.
The gun Bun-Bun lifts out of her bra
Fires, blinding the room, flashing delight, killing Miss
    Charlotte outright.
Now the sun is fully up hurrah.

Miss Charlotte thought she heard a scream,
And woke from her dream.
Then began to weep.
Then went back to sleep.

Kathryn Maris

Transference

I'm a cold girl.
I prefer a ghost in shoes to a man,
for ghosts can be filled.

Like this:
three buoys in the North Sea bend
towards a Dover beach.

I call them bodies. [I've filled them with a name.]
I want to swim out and save one
in a way

But the wind is cold
and the only sun on this stone beach
falls on me.

Street Sweeper

God scatters where he eats.
The sweeper wheels his cart to what falls.

The broom assembles a pile.
The wind dismantles the pile.

God is the messy wind. The pile
is the mouthpiece of the wind.

Sometimes the wind is bluster.
Sometimes the wind is a mute.

There is the God who listens.
There is the God who speaks.

The God who listens is a gentle liar.
The God who speaks is laconic and hard.

I ask if I'm loved.
He points to the graveyard his garden abuts.

I clutch his hair. I say *Am I loved?*
He claims his love for me is deep

but zealless. Over the garden wall,
the God who listens, the neighbour,

smiles when I ask if I am loved.
He points to the God across the wall,

the first God, the God I just left,
as if to say *God loves you.*

Sometimes he speaks through his dog.
Sometimes he doesn't speak.

If his mother tongue were 'dog'
or 'frog' or 'wind' or 'rubbish'

could I learn that language
and hear that I was loved?

Or would the answer
be something I couldn't hear.

The Periodic Table won't revoke
what it has put in the world –

earth metals, non-metals, catalysts.
It is God's slovenly generosity

and is difficult to gather,
as the street sweeper knows,

as the wind knows, as I know, and as God knows.
The sweeper smiles at me lovingly

like the silent god,
the one with the message I cannot hear.

Goddess

I love a bare world, like the world I strode with my boy.
I held his hand. I said, 'This is a *wall* of wind.' I flung

the words over the wall, but the wind-whirr deafened him.
His walk was a wrestle. The wan sky was his twin.

His father beckoned him to the swings
and the world grew barer. My son's love is a burden,

the Oedipal beat, beat, beat of his fist on his
father's tee-shirted chest. I see

that his leaving will repeat itself, and I will always let him leave.
And I love a bare world.

Once my husband named *me* as the goddess of all destruction.
I approved of that view. I view

myself that way, too: Queen of an Uninhabited Planet.
I tread on moon-rubble. Dust circles my knees.

My dress is Belgian deconstructionist. I am barefoot and regal
and unadorned but for the bracelet from the ward.

I am mother to all that is bare, all that is gone
for I have expected the bare world all along.

God Loves You

1 God's image was in the mirror and God's image was my grief. And lo, I knew I was not loved by Him and wept. And I knew shame. For though I was young, I was not young enough to weep in the face of the Lord who made me.

2 In sorrow, I set out. I prayed that God might look on me in my search for signs of love in His great world.

3 The first sign was clear: the call from Tom, Tom-Who-Loves-Me-Not. When he spoke unto me, he said three times, 'I love you,' and I knew it was He, for Tom is like God in sound and in grace. And that was a strong sign.

4 On the second day, there were finches in the air. I saw with my own eyes this flock yield the form of a heart before me.

5 The next sign, too, was full of meaning. It was a sign. And it was revealed to me thus: the Damut Estate. And in that name I read these words: *'Deus te amat.'*

6 On the road there was a child who pressed into my palm a yo-yo, where it was written: 'God loves you.' And I thanked the child, held him and wept, for he was righteous, and he was called Matthew. But still I was unloved.

7 For if God is in the mirror, and if God is the mirror of our world, then the signs will be false, for the world will reverse what God has shown me.

This is a Confessional Poem

I am guilty of so much destruction it hardly matters
anymore. There are so many thank-you notes I never wrote
that sometimes I'm relieved by the deaths of would-be
recipients, so I can finally let go of the shame.
I was awful to someone who was attached to the phrase
'social polish', as though she'd acquire it through repetition.
I took an overdose at a child's 6th birthday party.
I was born in a country which some have called
The Big Satan. I abandoned the country for one
that is called The Little Satan. I wished ill on a woman
who has known me for years and yet never remembers
who I am – and now she's involved in a public scandal.
I have been at parties where I was boring.
I have been at parties where I was deadly boring.
I have worn the wrong clothes to sacraments, not
for lack of outfits, but for a temporary failure of taste.
I'm a terrible, terrible liar, and everything I say is full of
misrepresentation. I once knew a very sweet girl
who stabbed herself in the abdomen 7 times.
She believed she was evil and thought 7 was a holy number.
Besides that she was sane, and told me her tale
out of kindness – because guilt recognizes guilt,
the way a mother can identify her own child.
I met her in a class called 'Poetry Therapy'
in which the assignment was to complete this statement:
When one door closes, another opens.
I wrote: *At the end of my suffering there was a door*,
making me guilty of both plagiarism and lack of imagination.
I was the vortex of suffering: present, future and retroactive

suffering. The girl tried to absolve me.
'Don't be Jesus,' she said. 'There are enough around here.'
I know I should thank her if she's alive,
but I also know it's unlikely I'll rise to the task.

It was a Gift from God

1 And the Lord said, 'Go to the woman who toils in the grove and give her this box.' And the angel asked not what was in the box, but delivered it to the woman.

2 The woman knew the ways of the Lord, so when she saw that the box was full of grief, she was not afraid.

3 God said, 'Take this grief, for it belonged to the One Who Came Before You, and she can bear it no longer. Take it to the East, as far as the next land.'

4 The woman did as God bid, but a soldier saw what she carried and threw her before the King.

5 The King asked, 'Why have you dishonoured our land with your beast?' She replied, 'It is not a beast, but a burden, and the Lord hath made *me* the beast of this burden.' The King was angry and said, 'Behold again the contents of your box!' She looked again and lo there was a beast where before there was none. For this she was locked away.

6 She prayed and the Lord was merciful. 'You were burdened with a beast and now you are captive like the beast. Go to the farthest sea and the beast will follow you, and there he will leave you for ever.'

7 So the lord sent an angel to open the prison door and it came to pass that

the woman was followed to the sea
by the beast who, when it was night,
fled to the dunes and withdrew from
this world.

On Returning a Child to Her Mother
at the Natural History Museum

Hello, my name is Kathryn and I've come
here to return your daughter, Emily.
She told me you'd suggested that she look
around upstairs in 'Earthquakes and Volcanoes',
then meet you and her brothers in the shop.
You know that escalator leading to
the orb? It's very long and only goes
one way, you can't turn round. She asked me if
I knew the way back down and would we come
with her into the earthquake simulator –
that reproduction of the grocery shop
in Kobe, where you see the customers
get thrown around with Kirin beer and soy
sauce, things like that. She told us stuff about
your family. Apparently you had
a baby yesterday! That can't be right:
you're sitting here without one and my God
your stomach's flat! She also said she'd had
an operation in the hospital
while you were giving birth one floor below.
I know, I know: kids lie and get confused,
mine do that too. She talks a lot. She's fat.
She may not be an easy child to love.
I liked her, though. I liked her very much,
and having her was great, the only time
all day my daughter hasn't asked me for
a dog! We got downstairs and funnily
enough we found your middle son. He ran
to us upset and asked us where you were.
But here you are – exactly where you said –
the shop! Don't worry: I don't ever judge

a mother. Look at me: my daughter drank
the Calpol I left out when she was two;
I gave my kids Hundreds and Thousands once
for dinner while I lay down on the floor,
a wreck. I know you well! Here's Emily.

Bright Day

Sometimes, but almost never,
when the light is Good
and the wind isn't wrong,
I say to the children, 'Look.'
And I make them stand, under God,
while the sky lords over their little minds
and I teach them to recognize
a 'God Day' when they see it.

But next time it happens,
they shout, 'It's a Mama Day!
She says she can see God.'
Every generation has its take on things.
My mother called it a Sunny Day.
Her mother called it a Day.

The Devil Got into Her

1 The woman appealed to the Doctor, for she could not be cured. The Doctor had the likeness of the Lord, and the Lord spoke through him: 'You are overcome by a demon. When it is slain, it will harm you no longer.'

2 The woman asked how the demon should be slain, and the Doctor said there was a man but that she must be the one to find him.

3 The woman found a man who said he could slay the demon, but he did not, for he was a demon himself and full of trickery. So the woman slew the man and was not punished, for the King of the land was glad to be rid of him.

4 She returned to the Doctor and told of her failure. 'Tell me the name of this demon that has made me its home.' But this he would not reveal.

5 So again she set out. An angel took the form of a crone and said, 'Find the man in the west whose name is "Slay".'

6 So the woman found that man and he said to her, 'God hath forbidden me to rid you of this demon. But in the city to the east there is a man who can help you.' And he told her where to find him.

7 The man in the east was kind, so the woman came to live with him. But he was kind to the demon too, for he did

not kill it, but placed it in a box. And the woman was healed, but still she feared the demon and viewed the box askance.

Darling, Would You Please Pick Up Those Books?

How many times do I have to say
get rid of the books off the goddamn floor
do you have any idea how it feels
to step over books you wrote about *her*
bloody hell you sadist what kind of man
are you all day long those fucking books

in my way for 3 years your *acclaimed* books
tell me now what do you have to say
for yourself you think you're such a man
silent brooding pondering at the floor
pretending you're bored when I mention *her*
fine change the subject ask, 'Do I feel

like I need more medication' NO I don't *feel
like I need more medication* it's the books
don't you see don't you see it's *her*
why don't you listen to anything I say
and for God's sake books on the floor
are a *safety hazard* remember that man

from Cork who nearly died fine that man
fell over a hurley not a book but I don't feel
you're getting the point the point is that a floor
is not an intelligent place for books
books *I* have to see and books that say
exactly where and how you shagged her

what shirt she wore before you shagged her
I can write a book too about some man
better still about *you* I can say
something to *demonize* you how would you feel

about *that* ha ha why don't I write a book
about how I *hoover your sodding floor*

and how you've *never once* hoovered your floor
why can't I be a muse why can't I be a 'her'
what does one have to do to be in a book
around here do I have to be *dead* for a man
to write me a poem how do you think it feels
to be non-muse material can't you say

you feel for me what you felt for her
can't you say I'm better than that woman
can't you get those books off the floor?

The Tall Thin Tenor

The tall thin tenor sings
The tall thin tenor sings to the young soprano
The young soprano sings the part of Poppea
The young woman Poppea has seduced the king
The tall thin tenor is king
The young soprano Poppea becomes the new young queen
The young soprano replaces the old queen Ottavia
The old queen Ottavia sings of replacement

The tall thin tenor sings over the soprano
The tall thin tenor sings over her to his small thin wife
His small thin wife holds a child in the stalls
His thin wife holds their quiet daughter
His small wife sings quietly to their daughter
The small wife is quiet when the queen sings

Last Supper

I asked for liver as it was the closest thing to poison.
He cooked it robotically in the scratched Teflon pan.
I sat at the table like the good girl I'd mainly been.

I tried to eat the liver but was ill with bile of my own.
He ate the liver and was quiet until it was done.

Then he said he was sick of being cast as a demon,
that I'd asked too many questions that resembled accusation,
and did I know I have a limitless need for affirmation.

I had things of my own to say, but why say them.
I thought of a cad whose headstone reads *Resurgam*
and how it's like a perverse joke

and how it must be easy to be a man who can say *Resurgam*
over a death sentence, a flame or a Teflon pan –
whereas I could hardly rise from the table again.

Will You Be My Friend, Kate Moss?

My daughter's in your daughter's ballet class.
I sat beside you at the Christmas show?
I really loved the outfit you had on!
Three years ago I tried to emulate
your look in *Grazia*: you can't believe
how hard it was to find some knee-high boots,
a tunic-dress, and earrings just like yours.
The icon of my generation, Kate,
you were The Waif – that's what we aimed to be –
and yet it's so unfair you got the blame
for all that teenage anorexia.
We'd never look like you no matter what:
I saw that when you walked into the class
(your daughter was ecstatic, by the way!)
your terrifying cheekbones mocking mine.
The line 'Alas, poor Yorick!' struck me then:
your head could easily be on Hamlet's palm!
And speaking of: I heard your friend Jude Law
is in New York reprising Hamlet at
the Broadhurst Theatre on 44th.
I miss New York – I wish that we could go.
I have this friend, Nuar, I'm sure you'd love:
she's smarter than the two of us combined,
and stunning, too, and has two little girls.
At Yaddo, where we met, she'd quote Foucault
and Nietzsche on the buffet line. She held
my hand one creepy night when we got lost
around the lake beside her studio.
I really miss Nuar, and Suki too,
whose sense of style is on a par with yours.
Let's all go out one night! I'll do my best
to stick with you despite the fact that I'm

a hypochondriac and petrified
of class A drugs. We have so many things
in common, like you're pretty much my age;
we share initials; the circumference of
our thighs is basically the same. (I checked.)
I also saw you surreptitiously
admire my silver space-age dress! You did!
Now that my daughter's been moved up a grade
will this be *adios amigo*, Kate?
She's not disconsolate about the change
but then she's at the age where all you say
is 'will you be my friend.' Remember that?

Number Plate Bible

B49 NSD
Banished

A4L BOT
Animal Boat

MO5E SRS
Moses Stutters

AB24 ABM
Absalom, Absalom

YM3 Jo8
Why Me, Said Job

BL77 MEE
Blessed Are the Meek

M15 H1R
Mary's Hair

JE56 WPT
Jesus Wept

ST2 PUL
St. Paul

TR6 66PS
Trumpets

Variations on Melissanthi's 'Atonement'

1. ATONEMENT

Every time I sinned a door half opened and the Angels
who never found me virtuous enough to be beautiful
tipped over the vase of flowers that was their souls.
Every time I sinned it was as though a door opened
and tears of compassion fell on the grass.
And though guilt chased me out of heaven like a sword,
every time I sinned a door half opened and though men
found me ugly, the Angels found me beautiful.

Melissanthi (Greek, 1910–1991)

2. ATONEMENT

My reasons for it:

1. Men found me beautiful; angels found me ugly.

2. Every time I thought I might be beautiful, the angels
said No.

3. Every time I opened the back door, my soul was there in the
grass, chased out of heaven – where I was not found beautiful.

4. When men gave me flowers, the angels were in the vase,
telling me I had sinned, my virtue was half full, and I was not
beautiful.

5. Even though I offered them my guilt, they held me off with
a door.

6. Every time I tipped to one side, my tears fell on an angel whose compassion blocked the door like a sword.

7. I want everyone to find me beautiful, even the angels.

3. ATONEMENT

Though we may imagine Angels to be beautiful, there is evidence to the contrary. For example, the Angel who wielded his fiery sword when he chased our Parents out of Eden would have been hideous! Equally, Angels may be less compassionate than we surmise; surely we, too, would abandon the notion of virtue if we glimpsed the sins of Man every time we dared open our door. How ugly our world must seem, how full of guilt! The things Man creates – a picture, a vase, even a Cathedral – shall never be half as beautiful as a flower that springs from the grass, or the rain that is God's own tears. We must tip our hats to the Angels; only they know why they abide us.

The House with Only an Attic and a Basement

The woman in the attic did not have visitors.

The man in the basement gave parties that were popular.

The woman in the attic had mononucleosis.

The man in the basement had type 1 diabetes.

The woman in the attic listened to audiobooks which the man in the basement held in disdain.

The door to the attic swelled in some weathers; in order to shut, it had to be slammed.

'There is a way in which' was a way in which the man opened sentences, as in 'There is a way in which to close a door so it doesn't slam.'

The woman in the attic took cautious walks to build her strength.

The man in the basement pointedly said, 'Some of us have ailments which are not manufactured.'

The man in the basement wrote stories about heroin.

The woman in the attic read stories with heroines.

The woman in the attic noticed a bruise that ran from the top to the base of her thigh.

The bruise looked like Europe.

The man in the basement was in love with the sister of the secretive man who loved him more.

He whooped at the woman, 'You killed your student?'

To himself he wept, 'I killed my father.'

The man in the basement, recently divorced, was left with literally two possessions.

The woman in the attic purchased books on psychopathology.

The man in the basement produced faecal matter
that blocked the pipes in both attic and basement.

The woman in the attic produced nothing at all.

The woman in the attic was a waste of space.

The man in the basement had sex almost daily.

The woman in the attic had panic attacks.
The man in the basement had only one rule:
the woman in the attic was banned from his bedroom.
But once she stole in and lay on his bed
in his absence (or perhaps he was absent because she was there).
The man in the basement moved to the West Coast;
the woman in the attic crossed the Atlantic,
whereas the house with the attic and basement saw states
of fumigation, exorcism, detoxification, and rehabitation.

Ladies' Voices

CURTAIN RAISER

Everyone has gone
But the barbecue is here. Is someone coming back for it?
William is going back for it tomorrow
Ah that belongs to William. William is going back tomorrow
What a successful weekend overall

Did anyone see a white china salad bowl
I'm looking for a plastic container with a red strip around
    the edge
Weren't we fortunate with the weather
Weren't we lucky
Wow what a race
What a race indeed

ACT II

Accident on the M4 by the exit to the M25
We're stuck in it too
We are through
I'm driving Rupert, Henry & the dog
Are you there yet?
You will be fine, I was caught too
The rain is driving at an angle
Where are you all?
We're all here, where are you?

ACT III

First Brexit, now this
What a week, so sad
I feel the way I did last Friday, totally bereft
Those boys are lucky with their great British strengths
Calm under pressure, humility & humour
Nick was telling us how he read *The Odyssey*

That will stand them in good stead

ACT IV

What a shame, big loss
It's a very difficult time
Equally painful
I saw them laughing

EPILOGUE

His father has been given one month to live
He's not ill at all
Does anyone have Nurofen?
Oh dear, was it raining?

Gosh I will miss it, and you, very much
Congratulations and best wishes for the future
What a fabulous memory
Wasn't it just such a special and wonderful occasion
The baton is well and truly passed

Singles Cruise

It was a singles cruise but it wasn't a singles cruise:
each participant simulated detachment but none
was actually single. Some, like the recently widowed,
were attached to ghosts. Others were legally attached
to a living person they once but no longer loved.
A surprising number loved their partners profoundly
while fearing said partners inhabited the category
of those who loved them no longer. These participants,
whose fears may or may not have been founded,
attempted to self-protect by labelling themselves single.
Soon a pattern emerged: those who feared abandonment
developed around them a planetary-like orbit
of potential new partners to whom they could not attach
because they were already attached. Such orbits lasted,
sometimes, for years. The orbiters went to self-help groups
and/or analysts and/or wrote letters to advice columnists.
Because they could not detach from their objects of unrequited
affection, they became the predominant clientele for future
singles cruises, unilaterally sustaining the singles cruise business.

Here is the Official Line on Attire

Gentlemen must wear lounge suits,
ladies must wear dresses with a
hemline below the knee, no trousers
of any description. Hats are customary
but not essential. Cash and cards
may be used for refreshments.
This extraordinary spectacle is one
of the best things Britain has given
the world: civilised conduct on land,
absolute brutality on the water.

The X Man

His superpower was that his testicles manufactured sperm
with exclusively X chromosomes & that was ironic because
not only was he a beast to women but his 40 baby girls grew
up seeking men like the father they barely saw unless they went
to his studio to be painted which wasn't OK with their mothers
who were not only jealous but guilty of giving birth to girls
who were products of an X chromosome-making monster
& would soon suffer at the hands of other monsters with X-
type sperm thereby assuring the continuation of suffering
& meanwhile all the girls became writers who slouched
from sitting at desks & being daughters & lovers of beasts.

Ooga-Booga Cento

After Frederick Seidel

A naked woman my age is a total nightmare.
When the doctor told me that I could have died
(what could be more pleasant than talking about people dying?)
which is dangerous, which I do not like.
I go to Carnegie Hall.
The joy is actually terrible.

Under an exophthalmic sky of stars
and a flock of Japanese schoolgirls waiting to be fucked,
I sense your disdain, darling.
Civilized life is actually about too much.
I am no longer human.
The crocodile king is dead.

How to be a Dream Girl not a Doormat about the 'Ex'

While the Doormat asks neurotic questions about his ex,
the Dream Girl looks at her watch if her man brings up the ex,
and if the man ever says, 'Everyone was in love with my ex,'
a Dream Girl won't ask for a photo, but if a photo of the ex
is provided, the Dream Girl won't demean the appearance of the ex
because her man will likely rush to his ex's
defence. The lesson is that when a man considers his ex
a prize, looks have little to do with it, for when a woman acts
like a prize a man can forget he's with a battleaxe.
What should you say when he asks questions about *your* ex?
Remember you're a prize, so you needn't report that your ex
stole appliances or defaulted on child support or that your ex
has a Mafioso brother doing time for racketeering or that your ex
is 'still stalking you' – because your man will not find these ex
stories charming, if he's classy, so what you say about your ex
is simply, 'We wanted different things' or, alternatively, 'My ex
and I went separate ways.' It's none of his business: your ex
and all the vicissitudes of your past, like the jewellery your ex

gave you which you pawned, or your violent fantasies about your ex
because inquiring minds *don't* need to know. Did you know that exes
are a common conversation topic among men: 'You remember my ex,
the one who snapped . . . ?' they might say, referring to the 'terrible' ex
who was 'possessed by demons' thus causing the inevitable ex-
tramarital affair? Of course he *never* had anything to do with his ex's
transformation, he was a perfect angel, but lo and behold, the ex-
orcist was suddenly required! Women believe these narratives and ex-
coriate themselves if they're Doormats, but love is beset by variables,
and Dream Girls must take control in this world of unknowns.

Angel, Katherine: Dream

I'm going to live in a big fuck-off castle
with Diane Lockhart, Alicia Florrick &
Kalinda Sharma from *The Good Wife*.
I believe @SarahGPerry & @msamykey
might like to be residents too. Books
will be written, justice will be served
(kinda), delicious meals will be cooked.
Occasional wild parties will roll in like
storms. There will be many wings, as
solitude & some fucking peace & quiet
are needed. I will go out regularly – say
every three weeks? – to round up some men.
Will Gardner & the cowboy ballistics expert
dude will visit on a monthly basis. Criteria
for residency: ambivalence about cohabitation
(esp. with men) & intense need for solitude
punctuated by bursts of hedonism. It will be
a creative castle, where work is paramount.
Pleasure will also be central. Key to the
enterprise will be a highly pragmatic &
non-judgemental approach to sexual needs.
You might think I'm joking. Wrong, buster!

Demon

'Good news,' said the doctor, 'it's a demon.'
I asked for its name: was it No One?
Was it Superego? He said it wasn't those
but he couldn't guess the name. 'Who knows,'
he said, 'It mightn't even be a demon.
It's what we call a "diagnosis by elimination".'
Explaining he couldn't operate,
the doctor said let's go ahead and medicate
the hell out of it, make it sleepy.
I named him 'Demon' after his identity.
I put him to sleep twice a day, one short,
one long; three times a week he did sport;
he grew to six foot two; I said he was good;
I went to the door of his room and left food.

The summer day the spike went into my

The summer day the spike went into my
brother's head, as such things happened
in the twentieth century when the Freudian
death drive was often accessed out of
boredom, I learned from my doctor parents
that scalps bleed profusely. Twenty years later,
when Theodore and Cosima jumped on little
Robert's bed and Theodore fell off and his
white-blond head turned red, I said, 'Scalps bleed
profusely' and Rachel, his mum, thanked me
for my composure. Robert's mum, Emily,
who had wanted to be a jazz singer or actress
and who always introduced me as a poetess,
said she knew a couple who had a second child
because their friends' child died in a freak accident.
But back to the summer day the spike
grazed my brother's scalp: I slept beside him
in his racing car bed and my father woke me
and slapped my face, thinking, I assume, of sex,
whereas I was already thinking about death.

Catherine and Her Wheel (III)

When my teachers grew old and died, when my friends
went sparer and sparer, when small islands suffered
from the New Weather, when my children found me
offensively morbid, when my looks officially went,
when my enemies became friends became rivals became
allies became masters became servants until we lacked
energy for anything even escape from our celebrated
cities whose skylines transitioned from greatness to perfect
meaninglessness as when a person loses her mind
like my cohorts who were going crazier and crazier until
I wondered *Is this sensitive ageing? What the fuck
is going on here?* . . . I knew nothing, and the nothing I knew
was more profoundly nothing even than the nothing
we know at our rarest bottommost humblest moments
because usually we know *one* thing – we know
we're not dead or that 'apple' has a feminine article in French,
but this was *absolute zero* like when the saint fell off a horse
then into a coma then woke up and said to another saint
that there was *nothing*, that there was *'nada de nada'*,
the most perfect Spanish expression, the most beautiful
and poetic circle, the nothing wheel,
the wheel I have carried through all routes of my life, the wheel
I was fundamentally wedded to, my true beloved,
watch me touch it now look at it look at it: nothing.

ACKNOWLEDGEMENTS

For material included in this selection the following grateful acknowledgements are made: to Faber & Faber for poems by Sam Riviere from *81 Austerities* (2012) and *Kim Kardashian's Marriage* (2015); to Sam Riviere for his poems from *Standard Twin Fantasy* (Egg Box Publishing, 2014) and *True Colours* (After Hours, 2016); to Farrar, Straus & Giroux for Frederick Seidel's poem 'Wanting to Live in Harlem', from *Poems 1959– 2009* (2009); to Faber & Faber for poems by Frederick Seidel from *Selected Poems* (2006), *Ooga-Booga* (2009), *Nice Weather* (2012) and *Widening Income Inequality* (2016); to Four Way Books for Kathryn Maris's poems from *The Book of Jobs* (2006); to Seren Books for Kathryn Maris's poems from *God Loves You* (2013); and to Kathryn Maris for poems from her forthcoming collection, *The House with Only an Attic and a Basement* (Penguin, 2018).

Other poems by Sam Riviere first appeared in *The Best British Poetry 2015* (Salt), *Poetry*, *The Poetry Review* and *The White Review*; by Frederick Seidel, in *The Paris Review*; and by Kathryn Maris, in *Magma*, *The Nation*, *Poetry*, *Poetry London*, *The Poetry Review*, *Poetry Wales*, *Swimmers* and *Traverse Poetry Trading Cards* (Stonewood Press).

Thanks are also due to Madeleine Plaut, words from whose emails are used in 'Here is the Official Line on Attire'.